Silly Shakespeare

MACBETH

PAUL LEONARD MURRAY

with help from

WILLIAM SHAKESPEARE

Alphabet
PUBLISHING

ISBN: 978-1-948492-74-4

For permission requests or discounts on class sets and bulk orders contact us at:

Alphabet Publishing
1204 Main Street #172
Branford, CT 06405 USA

info@alphabetpublishingbooks.com

www.alphabetpublishingbooks.com

For performance rights, please contact Paul Murray at paulplaying@gmail.com

Interior Formatting and Cover Design by Melissa Williams Design

For Daniel Mijič, the 11 year old family friend whose reading of the whole play inspired me to publish it.

Summary

Macbeth (or *The Tragedy of Macbeth* to give it its full title), believed to be first performed in 1606, is one of Shakespeare's most famous and widely performed plays. Some say that the play is cursed because of the way in which it portrays the witches and so tradition has it that the name of the play should not be spoken in theatre; instead it is referred to simply as 'the Scottish play'.

***

The Scottish play begins with the brief appearance of a trio of witches who act as the narrators for this version of the play, appearing between each scene. It then moves to a military camp, where the Scottish King Duncan hears the news that his generals, Macbeth, and Banquo, have defeated two separate invading armies—one from Ireland and one from Norway.

Following their battle with these enemy forces, Macbeth and Banquo encounter the witches as they cross a moor. The witches prophesise that Macbeth will be made Thane (a rank of Scottish nobility) of Cawdor and eventually King of Scotland. They also prophesise that Macbeth's companion, Banquo, will father a line of Scottish kings, although Banquo will never be king himself. The witches vanish, and Macbeth and Banquo treat their prophecies sceptically until some of King Duncan's men come to thank the two generals for their victories in battle and to tell Macbeth that he has indeed been named Thane of Cawdor. The previous Thane betrayed Scotland by fighting for the Norwegians and Duncan has condemned him to death.

Macbeth is intrigued by the possibility that the

remainder of the witches' prophecy—that he will be crowned king—might be true, but he is uncertain what to expect. He visits with King Duncan, and they plan to dine together at Inverness, Macbeth's castle, that night. Macbeth writes ahead to his wife, Lady Macbeth, telling her all that has happened.

Lady Macbeth suffers none of her husband's uncertainty. She desires the kingship for him and wants him to murder Duncan in order to obtain it. When Macbeth arrives at Inverness, she overrides all of her husband's objections and persuades him to kill the King that very night. He and Lady Macbeth plan to get Duncan's two servants drunk so they will black out; the next morning they will blame the murder on them, who will be defenceless as they will remember nothing. While Duncan is asleep, Macbeth stabs him, despite his doubts and a number of supernatural portents, including a vision of a bloody dagger. When Duncan's death is discovered the next morning, Macbeth kills the servants and easily assumes the kingship. Duncan's sons Malcolm and Donalbain flee to England and Ireland, respectively, fearing that whoever killed Duncan wants to kill them as well.

Fearful of the witches' prophecy that Banquo's heirs will seize the throne, Macbeth hires a group of murderers to kill Banquo and his son Fleance. They ambush Banquo on his way to a royal feast, but they fail to kill Fleance, who escapes into the night. Macbeth becomes furious: as long as Fleance is alive, he fears that his power remains insecure. At the feast that night, Banquo's ghost visits Macbeth. When he sees the ghost, Macbeth raves fearfully, startling his guests, who include most of the great Scottish nobility. Lady Macbeth tries to neutralize the damage, but Macbeth's kingship incites increasing resistance from his nobles and subjects.

Frightened, Macbeth goes to visit the witches again who show him a sequence of demons and spirits who present him with further prophecies: he must beware of Macduff, a Scottish nobleman who opposed Macbeth's accession to the throne; he is incapable of being harmed by any man born of woman; and he will be safe until Birnam Wood comes to Dunsinane Castle. Macbeth is relieved and feels secure, because he knows that all men are born of women and that forests cannot move. When he learns that Macduff has fled to England to join Malcolm, Macbeth orders that Macduff's castle be seized, and that Lady Macduff and her children be murdered.

When news of his family's execution reaches Macduff in England, he is stricken with grief and vows revenge. Prince Malcolm, Duncan's son, has succeeded in raising an army in England, and Macduff joins him as he rides to Scotland to challenge Macbeth's forces. The invasion has the support of the Scottish nobles, who are appalled and frightened by Macbeth's tyrannical and murderous behaviour.

Lady Macbeth, meanwhile, becomes plagued with fits of sleepwalking in which she bemoans what she believes to be bloodstains on her hands. Before Macbeth's opponents arrive, Macbeth receives news that she has killed herself. Nevertheless, he awaits the English and fortifies Dunsinane, to which he seems to have withdrawn in order to defend himself, certain that the witches' prophecies guarantee his invincibility. He is struck numb with fear, however, when he learns that the English army is advancing on Dunsinane shielded with branches cut from Birnam Wood. It looks like Birnam Wood is indeed coming to Dunsinane, fulfilling half of the witches' prophecy.

In the battle, the English forces gradually overwhelm his army and castle. On the battlefield, Macbeth encounters the vengeful Macduff, who declares that he was not "of woman born" but was instead "untimely ripped" from his mother's womb (what we now call birth by caesarean section). Though he realizes that he is doomed, Macbeth continues to fight until Macduff kills and beheads him. Malcolm now becomes the King of Scotland.

Playing Style

Although staying true to the original plot, characters, and scenes, this version of Macbeth brings humour to the Scottish play and as such the play lends itself to an exaggerated clownish/grotesque playing style. This does not mean to say that the tragedy of the original cannot be conveyed, but this will be done in a much more popular playing style than the traditional.

Unlike the original, this version of *Macbeth* is told through the eyes of the witches. It is their interventions in Scottish life that created the tragedy which they narrate directly to the audience. They are talking directly with the audience, meaning there is no fourth wall. In staging the play fun can be had by having the witches popping up at various places throughout the theatre (including the auditorium), thus adding to the sense of excitement and intimacy of the production.

As in the original, the supernatural elements of the production such as the floating dagger, the ghost and the apparitions will present the biggest directorial challenges (especially when working on a budget). I would advise experimenting in production with simple solutions: hanging the floating dagger on the end of a fishing pole held by a stagehand in full view for example. In order to maintain the 'spooky and gloomy' atmosphere it may be necessary to employ a dry-ice machine at various points throughout the play and a soundtrack should be used to indicate (for example) weather conditions, battle sounds, drums, and fanfares; however, if you wish, you may use the offstage cast to make sound effects 'live'.

On some occasions, you will find the rhyming scheme helpful to the playing, in which case the actors should just 'stand back', enjoy the words and help the audience do the same. On other occasions, the rhyming scheme will seem stifling and restrictive, in which case, do not be afraid to improvise a little, add your own occasional lines, or do not emphasise the rhymes so much.

Overall, this version should be fun to play and watch. It can be produced with a small budget and should be produced in an 'over the top' manner, which can give you a chance to play with your own ideas of theatricality.

Cast of Characters

DUNCAN:	*King of Scotland*
MALCOLM & DONALBAIN:	*his Sons*
MACBETH:	*Thane of Glamis*
BANQUO:	*General of the King's Army*
MACDUFF, LENNOX,	
ROSS, MENTEITH, ANGUS,	
& CAITHNESS:	*Noblemen of Scotland*
FLEANCE:	*Son to* BANQUO
SIWARD:	*Earl of Northumberland,*
	General of the English Forces
YOUNG SIWARD:	*his Son*
SEYTON:	*an Officer attending* MACBETH

Murderers
Boy, Son to MACDUFF
A Scottish Doctor
A Sergeant
A Porter
An Old Man

LADY MACBETH
LADY MACDUFF
HECATE *and Three Witches*
Messengers
The Ghost of BANQUO
Apparitions

Act I

SCENE I.

A desert place. Thunder and lightning.
(Enter three WITCHES*)*

FIRST WITCH
Welcome to the Scottish play.

SECOND WITCH
It's "Scottish" cos[1] it rains all day.

THIRD WITCH
It's cold enough to see your breath.

FIRST WITCH
We're waiting here to see Macbeth.

(Pause)

1—Abbreviation for because

SECOND WITCH
Hanging out in bogs[2] and ditches,

THIRD WITCH
Yes, you've guessed it; we're the witches!

FIRST WITCH
We're here to guide you all the way,

SECOND WITCH
Because we know the end of the play.

THIRD WITCH
We'll help you through the tricky bits,

SECOND WITCH
So you can keep hold of your wits!

THIRD WITCH
To kick things off, we've made a spell,

FIRST WITCH
And to Macbeth we three shall tell

SECOND WITCH
The things that we have seen he'll be,

THIRD WITCH
But we don't do that until scene three.

2—Swamps

FIRST WITCH
We're freezing here out on this heath[3]

SECOND WITCH
So we'll keep this first scene very brief.

THIRD WITCH
You'll leave us now and meet the King.

WITCHES
They've all just finished battling!

(Exeunt[4] all)

3—Grasslands

4—A word used in scripts to mean exit for more than one character/actor.

 SCENE II.

A military camp near Forres. The sounds of fighting.

(Enter DUNCAN, MALCOLM, DONALBAIN, LENNOX, ROSS
with Attendants, meeting a bleeding Sergeant)

DUNCAN
My son . . .

MALCOLM
. . . My King . . .

DONALBAIN
. . . My King . . .

DUNCAN
. . . My son
Tell me, are our battles won?

MALCOLM
This bloodied man knows everything.

DONALBAIN
Come over here and tell the King.

SERGEANT
The Irish came to take our land,

But Macbeth showed a steely[5] hand.
He ran into the field of battle
And killed them all like they were cattle.
And after that, 'bout half past two,
He killed all the Norwegians too.
I never saw such soldiers go
Like Macbeth and his mate Banquo.

DUNCAN
And what of the Cawdor thane[6]?

MALCOLM
Bad news there, Dad. Ask Donalbain.

DONALBAIN
He always wanted to be a Norse.

ROSS
He fought with them . . .

LENNOX
. . . he did . . .?

DUNCAN
. . . Of course!
Go find him now, cut off his head,
And make Macbeth that thane instead.

5—Strong and determined

6—A thane is a kind of Scottish lord and Cawdor is an area in Scotland.

LENNOX
He long deserved this big promotion.

ROSS
A man of true and rare devotion.[7]

DUNCAN
In times of boom, in times of bust,
Macbeth's a man we all can trust.

(Exeunt all)

7—Loyalty

SCENE III.

A heath near Forres. The sound of thunder.
(Enter the three WITCHES*)*

ALL
Hubble, bubble, toil and trouble.

FIRST WITCH
Get me a Scotch.

SECOND WITCH
Make mine a double.

THIRD WITCH
You sure Macbeth is on his way?
I can't be hanging out here all day.
I can barely feel my feet at all.

FIRST WITCH
I saw it in my crystal ball.

SECOND WITCH
My nose is cold, my eyes are weepy.

FIRST WITCH
Here they come, start looking creepy!

(Enter MACBETH *and* BANQUO*)*

MACBETH
I killed them here, I killed them there.

BANQUO
Macbeth, you killed them everywhere.

MACBETH
For my King; a goodly Scot!

BANQUO
They are witches, are they not?

MACBETH
Wrinkled skin and matted hair.
Bearded chins . . .

SECOND WITCH
 . . . and we don't care.

FIRST WITCH
We know you are the Thane of Glamis.

THIRD WITCH
I recognise your manly arms.

SECOND WITCH
But Cawdor's crown to you we bring.

FIRST WITCH
And shortly after, you'll be king.

BANQUO
I don't mean any disrespect,
But tell me what can I expect?

FIRST WITCH
Banquo, you are very loyal.

SECOND WITCH
But, unfortunately, you'll never be royal.

THIRD WITCH
Your kids, however, when they're grown,
Will sit upon the Scottish throne.

(Pause)

MACBETH
From where do you three get this stuff?
I'm Thane of Glamis, and that's enough

BANQUO
Tell us how he will be king,
Then tell us more about my thing.

FIRST WITCH
Sorry, love, we've got to go.

SECOND WITCH
Cos basically that's all we know.

THIRD WITCH
Just wait and see what fates will come.

SECOND WITCH
I gotta go and warm my bum.

(WITCHES vanish)

BANQUO
They've gone, they've left, they've vanished, fled.

MACBETH
Do you believe a word they said?

BANQUO
To be a king you shouldn't strive.
The Thane of Cawdor's still alive.

(Enter ROSS *and* ANGUS*)*

ROSS
We left the King's impressive shack
With this here note to read to Mac

ANGUS
The Thane of Cawdor's popped his clogs.[8]
Now you will get to wear his togs.[9]

MACBETH
(*aside*) That's just what the old ladies said:
Now I am Cawdor cos he's dead.
Banquo, do you think it's true?

BANQUO
What those witches said to you?
I don't know, we'll have to see,
That's two things right; two out of three!

8—An idiom that means to die

9—Literally, clothes

MACBETH

If it's meant to be, it probably will.

(aside) The King is not a man to kill.

ROSS

Away my lords, the King awaits.

BANQUO

And so do all the tempted fates!

(Exits)

FIRST WITCH

I thought that all went very well.

SECOND WITCH

Already Cawdor! Well, who could tell?

THIRD WITCH

That news will start to play on his brain,

SECOND WITCH

As we go to the King again!

 SCENE IV.

Inside the palace at Forres. Trumpet fanfare.

(Enter DUNCAN, MALCOLM, DONALBAIN,
LENNOX, *and Attendants)*

DUNCAN
Is Cawdor dead?

MALCOLM
. . . He is that, Dad.

DUNCAN
I trusted him, the dirty cad
I hate to kill but need's a must.

(Enter MACBETH, BANQUO, ROSS *and* ANGUS*)*

Now there's a man that I can trust!
Welcome soldier, noble Lord–or
Should I call you Thane of Cawdor??
And I don't know if you got the hints,
But Malcolm, son, you're now a Prince.

*(*BANQUO *coughs)*

And mighty Banquo, hero too!
I reward you with a big . . . thank you!

MACBETH
A big 'thank you'! Well, isn't that nice?

BANQUO
My loyalty, sir, doesn't come with a price!

MALCOLM
Let's celebrate at Macbeth's castle.
We'll play 'musical chairs' or 'pass the parcel'.

DONALBAIN
Let us all to Inverness!

MACBETH
I'll head off first. It's a bit of a mess.
(*aside*) Now Malcolm is the next in line
To take the crown that could be mine
If I could just get rid of him.
My mind is dark, my thoughts are grim.
It's never right to take a life.
I'd best go home and tell the wife.

(He exits)

MALCOLM
What a wonderful man, Cawdor's new thane.

DONALBAIN
Your decisions are wise . . .

BANQUO
And long may you reign![10]

DUNCAN
Now let us exeunt to his place in the sticks
It's twenty-five miles on the A96.

> *(Trumpet fanfare. Everyone but the* WITCHES *exits)*

SECOND WITCH
So off we go to Macbeth's place.

THIRD WITCH
Where we shall see the lovely face

FIRST WITCH
Of Lady M, a delicate flower.

THIRD WITCH
Cometh the woman, cometh the hour!

10—Rule as king

SCENE V.

Inverness. Macbeth's castle.
(Enter LADY MACBETH, *reading a letter)*

LADY MACBETH
A letter from my husband Mac
To tell me when he's coming back.
He really is considerate.
Excuse me while I read a bit:
"I killed some men . . . I met the King
I played some golf" . . . the usual thing . . .
"I met some women," Oh, did he indeed?
"They told me some stuff and sparked off my greed . . ."
Ba blah ba blah ba blah ba blah
". . . That I will be king and I will go far!"
To be the king, he'll pay a price,
But he won't do it; he's far too nice.
And that's where Lady M comes in;
I'll practically do anything.

(Enter a breathless MESSENGER*)*

I wish you'd knocked. You gave me a fright.

MESSENGER
The King is coming here tonight!

LADY MACBETH
Coming here? But why? With who?

MESSENGER
They come to dine with all the crew:
Malcolm, Banquo, Donalbain,
The King, of course . . .

LADY MACBETH
. . . Is he insane?
Now walk away while you still can.
(aside) I have to start my evil plan.

(Exit MESSENGER)

A fiendish scheme . . . a devil's treaty
I'll sell my soul . . .

(Enter MACBETH)

. . . Oh, hello sweety!

MACBETH
Duncan's coming very soon.

LADY MACBETH
When will he leave . . . ?

MACBETH
. . . Tomorrow noon.

LADY MACBETH
He'll never leave. I have a plan:
We'll kill him here,

MACBETH

. . . You can't . . .

LADY MACBETH

. . . I can.

It's serious to kill a king

But I will think of everything.

Just look after your noble guest.

Prepare him for his final rest.

(Exits)

THIRD WITCH

At Macbeth's place, a plan contrived[11]

FIRST WITCH

And just in time . . . the King's arrived.

11—Made

SCENE VI.

In front of Macbeth's castle.

(Enter DUNCAN, MALCOLM, DONALBAIN, BANQUO, LENNOX, MACDUFF, ROSS, ANGUS, *and Attendants)*

DUNCAN
This castle has a lovely ceiling.

BANQUO
A classy place, a friendly feeling.

DUNCAN
And here she is, our lovely host.

LADY MACBETH
For all of our gifts to you I toast.

DUNCAN
Nonsense, dear. Your man's a winner.

LADY MACBETH
Shall we all go through for dinner?

(Exeunt all)

SCENE VII.

MACBETH'S *castle.*

*(In a hall outside the dining room, waiters and servants pass
by with trays,* MACBETH *enters from the feast)*

SECOND WITCH
The castle guests, they eat with vim.[12]

FIRST WITCH
But Macbeth's plan is eating him.

MACBETH
That really was a lovely spread
But I can't go kill old Duncan dead.
Maybe if no one ever found out
But with something like this, there's always a doubt.

(Enter LADY MACBETH*)*

LADY MACBETH
What are you doing in this part of the house?

MACBETH
I'm changing my mind . . .

12—Energy

LADY MACBETH
. . . Are you man or a mouse?

MACBETH
I worry, my love, that we will get caught.

LADY MACBETH
I said not to fret.[13] Now here's what I thought:
Tonight I'll get his servants drunk,
Then you'll go in and stab old Dunc.
Bloody the servants when hearing their snores.
Go back to bed, then early doors.[14]
Go wake them up and just be candid:
Tell them they've been caught red-handed.

MACBETH
You're ten times the man that I'll ever be
And I like your plan, it works for me.
I am resolved, I'll do the deed.
Now go back in and get a feed.

(Exeunt all)

13—Worry

14—To wake up early

Act II

SCENE I.

Court of MACBETH'S *castle.*

THIRD WITCH
They ate, they drank, they're all well fed.

FIRST WITCH
And now they're all tucked up in bed.

SECOND WITCH
All apart from Banquo and his son,

FIRST WITCH
Who are up keeping watch on 'battlement[15] one'?

(Enter BANQUO, *and* FLEANCE *bearing a torch before him)*

BANQUO
Hello, Fleance . . .

15—A wall on top of a castle

FLEANCE
... Oh hello, Dad

BANQUO
It's bitter cold ...

FLEANCE
... It's not that bad.

BANQUO
I couldn't sleep, I had bad dreams
But everything is quiet it seems.

FLEANCE
It's very dark but all seems fair.

      (Enter MACBETH, *and a* SERVANT *with a torch)*

But wait a minute. Who goes there?
Show yourself ...

BANQUO
... Friend or foe?

MACBETH
It's me, Macbeth. And you ...?

BANQUO
... Banquo.
You're thinking of what the witches said?
Is that what got you out of bed?
I can't but think it's coming true

MACBETH

Don't let it get a hold of you.

Just stick with me you'll be all right.

Now go and enjoy the rest of your night.

(Exeunt BANQUO, FLEANCE, *and* SERVANT*)*

MACBETH

Is that a dagger[16] in the air?

Covered all with blood and hair?

It floats alone for me to see.

I think this is a prophecy.

Death does for a body press

In this wintry Inverness.

(A bell rings)

The bell it tolls. The King I'll find

Before I go and change my mind.

(Exeunt all)

16—A kind of knife

SCENE II.

Court of MACBETH'S *castle.*

SECOND WITCH
I didn't do the dagger trick.

FIRST WITCH
And nor did I, his mind is sick!

SECOND WITCH
His wife is too . . .

THIRD WITCH
. . . She is indeed.

FIRST WITCH
I wonder if he's done . . .

WITCHES
. . . 'the deed'.

(Enter LADY MACBETH*)*

LADY MACBETH
The weather still is dark and foggy.
The King he sleeps, his servants groggy.
It's all set up for Mac the knife

To slip inside and take his life.
Was that a scream? A man or owl?

MACBETH
(*offstage*) Who goes there? Fair or foul?

LADY MACBETH
Alack, I'm scared we've been undone.
A better job I would have done.
Asleep he looked just like my dad
I may be evil, but not that bad.

>   *(Enter* MACBETH *with knives in hand and*
>   *blood on his clothes.)*

Here's my man! Did you succeed?

MACBETH
Yes, my dear. I've done the deed.

LADY MACBETH
You've killed the dad of Malc and Blain,
But you have to go back in again.

MACBETH
I can't revisit the attack.

LADY MACBETH
You've got to put the daggers back.

>   *(*MACBETH *looks at his hands)*

MACBETH

I heard a voice cry, 'Sleep no more!'
I left the room; they meant Cawdor!

LADY MACBETH

Give them to me and go to bed,

(Takes daggers from MACBETH*)*

And keep those voices out of your head.

(She exits. The sounds of knocking offstage.)

MACBETH

Who's there? Who knocks? And what's your story?
I'm covered in blood; my hands are gory.
I'll rinse them off, but I do doubt
The water'll get the blood all out.

(Re-enter LADY MACBETH*)*

LADY MACBETH

My hands are now like yours: all red.
Let's finish here and go to bed.

MACBETH

You hear the knock . . .?

LADY MACBETH

. . . The southern gate.
To our bedroom, there we'll wait
In our pyjamas killing time
Till someone comes across the crime.

So no more of this hocus-pocus.
Just keep your calm and keep your focus.

MACBETH

(Knocking offstage)

Another knock. I wish it were
Loud enough to Duncan stir!

SCENE III.

Court of MACBETH'S *castle.*

FIRST WITCH
Oh dear, oh dear, Macbeth is ruing.[17]

SECOND WITCH
I think I see some trouble brewing.

FIRST WITCH
Macduff and Lennox are on their way.

THIRD WITCH
Expecting just a normal day!

(Exeunt)

(Knocking offstage. Enter a PORTER. *A bit tipsy)*

PORTER
Early morning, half past four.
Who's that knocking on heaven's door . . .?
(Calls) I'm not St. Peter,[18] just a porter,
A family man: wife, son, one daughter.

17—Feeling regret

18—By tradition, Saint Peter is the doorman in Heaven.

It brings on quite a lot of stress
Working nights in Inverness.
That's why I like a little whisky,
But I'm not drunk . . . just a little tipsy.
I've got to keep my wits 'bout me.
You've heard about our V.I.P.?

(Knocking)

When you stay here with men and horses,
I keep away all evil forces.
I keep you safe from any stalker.
Just me and my mate, Johnnie Walker.[19]

(Opens the door. Enter MACDUFF *and* LENNOX*)*

MACDUFF
Hello, my friend. Were you awake?

PORTER
Oh fully sir, for Duncan's sake.
From November thru October,
I'm always here, alert and sober.

MACDUFF
Your nose is red, your eyes are shot,
You've had a drink . . . !

PORTER
 . . . But not a lot.
We may live in obscurity

19—A brand of whisky

But I am top security.
If anything bad did happen near,
I would be the last to hear.

MACDUFF
I think you'd mean you'd be the first.
Here comes Macbeth, go quench your thirst.

PORTER
Macbeth awake? That's a surprise!
I'll just nip off and rest my eyes.

(Exit PORTER. *Enter* MACBETH*)*

MACBETH
Good Lennox and my man Macduff.
I heard you knock . . .

MACDUFF
 . . . Not loud enough

LENNOX
We were waiting there about a year.

MACBETH
Sorry 'bout that. Why are you here?

MACDUFF
Duncan said to wake him up.

MACBETH
The King sleeps like a buttercup!

LENNOX

We've got his crown and packed the cart.

He likes to get an early start.

MACBETH

He's inside sleeping like a rock.

I'll go and give his door a knock.

MACDUFF

I'll go inside, out here is grim.

You've already done enough for him!

(He exits)

LENNOX

Chilly morning . . .

MACBETH

. . . Winter's grip.

You're looking tired, how was your trip?

LENNOX

I never saw a night so foul

The rain did lash, the wind did howl,

The earth did crack, the trees did shake,

Those in their graves they did awake.

Fires from the devil's well,

Something stirring deep in hell.

I have to tell you true, Macbeth.

I swear I heard the screams of death.

MACBETH

That's strange. I never heard a peep.

I had a truly restful sleep.

Early to bed and early to rise!

(Re-enter MACDUFF*)*

MACDUFF

King Duncan's dead . . .!

MACBETH

 . . . Oh, what a surprise!

MACDUFF

He lies there all bloody. You cannot conceive.

MACBETH

And in our spare room. It is hard to believe!

MACDUFF

There's blood on the rug, on the bed, and the shelves.

MACBETH

Wait here a sec. We'll go look for ourselves.

(Exeunt MACBETH *and* LENNOX*)*

MACDUFF

Sound the alarm. Everybody awake.

Get out of bed, for goodness sake.

Banquo and Malcolm, young Donalbain!

You won't be seeing your father again.

Rise up, rise up, like the hounds from hell.

And where is that Porter? Start ringing the bell.

(Bell rings. Enter LADY MACBETH*)*

LADY MACBETH
I'm here. What's up? What's all the rumpus?

MACDUFF
We've all just lost our moral compass
O gentle lady, how to say . . .

(Enter BANQUO*)*

LADY MACBETH
Banquo, you're here . . .

MACDUFF
 . . . and don't go away
Did you not hear? The King is dead.

LADY MACBETH
Murdered in our guestroom bed!

BANQUO
Murdered? Here . . . ?

MACDUFF
(to LADY MACBETH*)* . . . How did you know?

BANQUO
Oh cruel fate, say it's not so!

(Re-enter MACBETH *and* LENNOX, *with* ROSS*)*

MACBETH

It's so, it's so, a hideous sight.

A saintly man has died tonight.

(Enter MALCOLM *and* DONALBAIN*)*

DONALBAIN

What's going on? It's not yet eight . . .

MACDUFF

It's something bad . . .

DONALBAIN

. . . Just tell me straight.

MACDUFF

Your dad is dead . . .

LADY MACBETH

A crying shame . . .

MALCOLM

And do we know who is to blame?

MACBETH AND LADY MACBETH

His guards . . .

LENNOX

. . . so shocked, they didn't look well.

MACBETH

They were covered with blood, as guilty as hell

LADY MACBETH
So what did you do . . .?

MACDUFF
Yes, come on, I am curious.

MACBETH
I killed then both there.
I was mad . . .

LENNOX
 . . . He was furious.

MACDUFF
But what of a trial before they departed?

LADY MACBETH
Over here, boys. I'm feeling faint-hearted . . .

(She looks like she will faint)

MALCOLM
(*Aside to* DONALBAIN) It is not safe here. Let's run away.

DONALBAIN
(*Aside to* MALCOLM) A sound idea, without delay.

BANQUO
Some of us have work to do
Please move and let the lady through.

*(*LADY MACBETH *is carried out)*

MACDUFF
(Aside to DONALBAIN*)* Shortly we will find the reason
For this dark, cold-blooded treason.

LENNOX
All for one, and one for all

MACBETH
We'll meet up later in the hall.

(Exeunt all but MALCOLM *and* DONALBAIN*)*

MALCOLM
While they've gone, we two should split.
I do not trust these guys one bit.

DONALBAIN
To Ireland now, I think I'll flee.

MALCOLM
And how long for . . .?

DONALBAIN
. . . Don't know, we'll see.

MALCOLM
To England, I will travel forth,
Until it's safe to come back North.

DONALBAIN
I hope we'll meet back here one day,
When evil has been chased away.

(Exeunt all)

 SCENE IV.

Outside MACBETH'S *castle.*

FIRST WITCH
An eventful scene to say the least.

SECOND WITCH
Looks like Macbeth's become a beast.

FIRST WITCH
Steely-eyed and icy-hearted.

THIRD WITCH
And outside the castle, the gossip has started.

(Enter ROSS *and an* OLD MAN*)*

OLD MAN
For 80 years, I've been a Scot
But a night like that I remember not.
Blood and gore, unholy scenes,
Nothing is quite what it seems.

ROSS
I'm nowhere near as old as you,
But this here night does scare me too.

OLD MAN
I have to say you look quite rough.

ROSS
I'm waiting for my cousin Duff

(Enter MACDUFF)

Do we yet know who did the deed?

MACDUFF
The guards Mac killed. We all agreed

ROSS
But why would those two want Dunc dead?

MACDUFF
Malc and Donal both have fled.
But before they went across the border,
The King's two sons, they gave the order.
We think they gave the guards some cash
To give their poor old dad a slash.

ROSS
And when they get back into town
They hope to take their father's crown.

MACDUFF
But the crown's gone to Macbeth instead.
They've gone to put it on his head
In the little town of Scone.

ROSS
And where has Duncan's body gone?

MACDUFF
They've gone to put him in the ground.

ROSS
And what of you? You'll stick around?

MACDUFF
I'm heading back to my place in Fife,
And hoping for a quiet life.

ROSS
I, too, will leave this situation
And head off to the coronation.

MACDUFF
I go and just hope that somehow,
Our worst days are behind us now!

ROSS
Well, wait for me. We'll leave together.

OLD MAN
I'll wish for you more clement[20] weather.

            *(*ROSS *and* MACDUFF *exit)*

Thank God! They've gone, you never know
Just who is friend and who is foe.[21]
Will we find out who killed the King?
It's all rather unsettling.

            (Exeunt all)

20—Mild, pleasant

21—Enemy

Act III

Scene I.

Forres. The palace.

FIRST WITCH
Macduff's upset by all the malice.

SECOND WITCH
Banquo's now talking in the palace.

THIRD WITCH
About Macbeth who's hatched a plan.

FIRST WITCH
And on his own . . .

SECOND WITCH
. . . A sneaky man!

(Enter BANQUO)

BANQUO
Those witches! Well, their words came true!

And now he's King and Cawdor too.
But as it happened recently,
I think: did he act decently?
Ambition, it can turn your head
Next thing you know King Duncan's dead.
Talking of witches, remember my lesson?
Not me, but my sons are next in succession?
My head it spins with this perilous boast.
But I'll say no more here, or I could be toast!

(Trumpets fanfare. Enter MACBETH *as king,*
LADY MACBETH *as queen,* LENNOX, ROSS, *Lords,*
Ladies, and Attendants)

MACBETH
Here he is . . .you sleep all right?

BANQUO
Not too bad . . .

LADY MACBETH
 . . . You'll stay tonight?

BANQUO
I will, but first I'm going riding.

MACBETH
You know the princes are in hiding?

LADY MACBETH
Down south and west, I hear they flew
And telling tales 'bout you-know-who.

MACBETH
Talking of sons, your Fleance around?

LADY MACBETH
A fine young man with his feet on the ground.

BANQUO
His future is bright: that, no one can scupper.[22]

MACBETH
We agree with you there . . .

LADY MACBETH
 . . . see you back here for supper.

(Exeunt all but MACBETH, *and an attendant)*

What a lovely man that Banquo is:

He's kind and strong, the future's his.

He's moral with integrity. And that is just what worries
me.

ATTENDANT
Excuse me, your highness. There's men at the gate.

They look pretty dodgy. I told them to wait.

MACBETH
Nice work, MacDougal, show them in.

Then wait there 'til they leave again.

(Enter Murderers)

Did you give any thought to killing Banquo?

22—Stop or put an end to

MURDERER 2

Of course we did. We'll give it a go.

MURDERER 1

Lucky for you our lives are so sad.

MURDERER 2

You name it, we'll do it, no matter how bad.

MACBETH

That's great news, chaps, cos you've probably missed
That this morning I've added his son to the list.

MURDERER 1

The more the merrier is what we say.

MACBETH

And they've both gone out riding so do it today!

MURDERER 2

Think no more about it . . .

MURDERER 1

. . . Consider it done

MURDERER 2

It's all part of the service at MacMurderer and son!

(Exeunt all)

SCENE II.

The palace.

FIRST WITCH
He's employing some others to take him a life.

SECOND WITCH
But this time around he won't tell the wife!

(Enter LADY MACBETH*)*

LADY MACBETH
I just can't decide what napkins to use . . .
What's the matter, my dear? You don't look amused.

MACBETH
I don't really care for supper tonight.
Being king's upset my appetite.

LADY MACBETH
You worry too much; just relax and have fun.

MACBETH
We've done evil things . . .

LADY MACBETH
 . . . But what's done here is done!

MACBETH
Just one more thing . . .

LADY MACBETH
. . . Is it happening soon?

MACBETH
If all goes to plan, by late afternoon.

(Exeunt all)

SCENE III.

A park near the palace.

THIRD WITCH
Banquo's gone riding, his son by his side . . .

FIRST WITCH
In a dark little space, the MacMurderers hide!

(Enter three MURDERERS)

FIRST MURDERER
Another job for MacMurderer and son.

SECOND MURDERER
For murders in Scotland, we're still number one.

FIRST MURDERER
I thought that we were two, not three.
What are you doing here?

THIRD MURDERER
 . . . Macbeth sent me.

FIRST MURDERER
If it's alright with him, then it's alright with us.

SECOND MURDERER
Just follow our lead and don't cause a fuss.

FIRST MURDERER
What time are they due?

SECOND MURDERER
. . . 'bout late afternoon.

(Enter BANQUO, *and* FLEANCE *with a torch)*

THIRD MURDERER
Look, here they come now . . .

FIRST MURDERER
. . . Sit down, you buffoon!

BANQUO
. . . And that is how we killed the Swedes.

FLEANCE
Tell me more about your deeds.

BANQUO
We killed them first, and then the Norses.

FIRST MURDERER
When I say 'go', just grab their horses.

FLEANCE
They retreated back beyond Oslo?

BANQUO
Indeed, they did . . .

FIRST MURDERER
. . . GO GO GO GO!!!

(SECOND MURDERER *and* THIRD
MURDERER *set upon* BANQUO)

BANQUO
Who is this disturbing us?

FLEANCE
Dad, I think they're murderers!

BANQUO
Run, my lad, don't wait for me!
Flee, fly, free Fleance flee fly free . . .!

(*Dies.* FLEANCE *escapes. Darkness.*)

FIRST MURDERER
Give 'em the Glaswegian kiss.[23]

SECOND MURDERER
I've killed me one . . .

THIRD MURDERER
. . . I didn't miss.

FIRST MURDERER
Our job is done.

SECOND MURDERER
That's very nice.

23—A headbutt

FIRST MURDERER

(Moves to the scene of the murder)

You idiots, you've killed him twice.
The second one has run away.

SECOND MURDERER
Gone to fight another day.

THIRD MURDERER
One out of two, that ain't so bad.

SECOND MURDERER
We missed the son . . .

THIRD MURDERER
 . . . But got the dad!

FIRST MURDERER
The King, I'm sure this won't amuse
I'll go inside and share the news!

(Exeunt all)

SCENE IV.

A hall in the palace.

THIRD WITCH
Back in the palace, they continue as normal

FIRST WITCH
The Queen's prepared lunch . . .

SECOND WITCH
 . . . Very fancy and formal.

(A table set for a feast. Enter MACBETH, LADY MACBETH, ROSS, LENNOX, *Lords, and Attendants)*

MACBETH
Noble lords, please take your seats
And help yourself to all our treats.

LORDS
Thanks a lot, Macbeth, our king.

LADY MACBETH
Now make sure you eat everything.

LORDS
We will, our Queen . . .

LADY MACBETH
. . . They're very sweet.

(FIRST MURDERER *appears at the door*)

FIRST MURDERER
A word, my King . . .?

MACBETH

(*To* LADY MACBETH)

. . . Stay here and eat.

(*To the* MURDERER)

Your job is done? Is Banquo slain . . .?

FIRST MURDERER
You won't be seeing him again.

MACBETH
And what about his little son?

FIRST MURDERER
Well that is where we came undone.
He flowed, he flewed . . .

MACBETH
. . . He got away?

FIRST MURDERER
It don't sound good when it's said that way.

MACBETH
With Fleance free, I cannot rest.

FIRST MURDERER
I know that, sir. We did our best.

MACBETH
Well don't go far. We'll deal with this later
And if anyone asks, just say you're a waiter.

(Exit MURDERER*)*

LADY MACBETH
There he is: our royal host.
Come over here and make a toast.

MACBETH
Eat and drink, be of good cheer.

LADY MACBETH
That's quite enough. Sit down, my dear.

MACBETH
Is Macduff here? I asked for him.

ROSS
To miss this spread, 'tis shame on him.

LENNOX
He's probably just nipped to town.

LADY MACBETH
Oh please, your highness, just sit down.

(The GHOST OF BANQUO *enters, and sits
in* MACBETH'S *place)*

MACBETH
The table's full . . .

LENNOX
. . . Look, here's a chair.

MACBETH
There's no more space . . .

LADY MACBETH
. . . Just sit down there! *(Pointing to where* BANQUO *is sitting)*

MACBETH
From whence did come this ghost? From Hell?

LORDS
It's not from us . . .

ROSS
. . . The King's not well.

LADY MACBETH
The King is prone to little fits.

(To MACBETH) What's wrong with you? You've lost your
    wits!

MACBETH
In my chair . . . a bloody sight!

LADY MACBETH
Oh please calm down. You'll be alright.

You get like this when you are stressed.
It's something that should be addressed.

MACBETH
I told you 'bout that knife I saw.

LADY MACBETH
That's what I mean, you're feeling raw.

MACBETH
(*to the* GHOST) Now you've appeared, speak in this room!
Why doesn't our victim just stay in his tomb?
I've killed many men, a lot of times gory.
But reincarnation's a whole different story.

(GHOST OF BANQUO *vanishes*)

LADY MACBETH
For the last time, sit down. You shake like a lassie.
You're supposed to be king. You're supposed to be classy.

MACBETH
Sorry lads for the digression,
Just a little indigestion,
And so to make good my amends
Let us toast to absent friends.

LORDS
To all those folks from way back when
And yesterday . . .

(*Re-enter* GHOST OF BANQUO)

MACBETH

. . . It's back again!

LADY MACBETH

(To the lords) Excuse my husband, he's under the weather

(To MACBETH*)* And I'm telling you now, I'm at the end of
    my tether!

MACBETH

I am a braver man than most,

But I don't know how to fight a ghost.

              (GHOST OF BANQUO *vanishes)*

And now he's gone! He's always leaving!

LADY MACBETH

Well done, my King. You've ruined the evening.

MACBETH

It wasn't me that spoiled the night.

You all did see this terrible sight.

ROSS

What sight, my lord . . .?

LENNOX

. . . It's in his head!

LADY MACBETH

That's it, my lords. It's time for bed.

Just leave the food and don't look back.

We'll sort you out a little snack.

LENNOX
Get better soon, Macbeth, goodnight

LADY MACBETH
And mind your bedbugs they don't bite!

(Exeunt all but MACBETH *and* LADY MACBETH)

MACBETH
You know they say 'the dead shall rise
To haunt the one who took their eyes'?
They curse a man and steal his wit,
That could be me . . . What time is it?

LADY MACBETH
It's late my dear. The light is dim.

MACBETH
And where's Macduff? I sent for him.

LADY MACBETH
He hasn't done what you commanded.

MACBETH
He'll be sorely reprimanded.
Being king is full of glitches.
Tomorrow, I will see the witches.
Will this end? I must know how.
We've come too far to turn back now.
So many tasks, both big and small.

LADY MACBETH
And when we wake, we'll do them all.

MACBETH

To sleep, to dream, unconscious bliss.

LADY MACBETH

Don't worry. You'll get used to this.

(Exeunt all)

SCENE V.

A Heath. Thunder.

(Enter the three WITCHES *meeting* HECATE*)*

THIRD WITCH
I heard our names. I think we're due.

SECOND WITCH
And our boss Hecate's coming, too.

FIRST WITCH
Sometimes that's good, sometimes it's bad.

THIRD WITCH
Depending how much fun we've had . . .

FIRST WITCH
Hubble, bubble, toil and fear . . .

SECOND WITCH
Look lively now, the boss is here!

FIRST WITCH
Such a bleak, unholy place.

HECATE
The ideal spot to show my face.

SECOND WITCH

I've still got problems with my eyes.

FIRST WITCH

To what do we owe this little surprise?

HECATE

I've told you three a thousand times:
Be careful where you share your rhymes.
Never tell your declarations
To a man with hallucinations!

SECOND WITCH

We're sorry, chief. We got it wrong.

HECATE

Meet me tomorrow at Acheron.
Macbeth will come to hear some more
Of what the future has in store.
We'll tie him up in such confusion
With prediction and illusion,
He'll laugh at death and feel secure
And that will seal his fate for sure.
So meet me there and bring your cauldron.

SECOND WITCH

The one we got from Saffron Walden?

HECATE

Bring all the things that you can beg
To bring this Scotsman down a peg.

FIRST WITCH
Before you go, you'll share a brew?

HECATE
I need to leave . . . and so do you!

(Exit HECATE*)*

SECOND WITCH
I knew we should have got permission,

THIRD WITCH
Before our little Scottish mission.

(Exeunt all)

SCENE VI.

Forres. The palace.

FIRST WITCH
Meanwhile in the palace, where they have got heating,

SECOND WITCH
Young Lennox is having a secretive meeting.

(Enter LENNOX *and another Lord)*

LENNOX
I hear you are a popular knight.
You saw Macbeth act weird tonight.
And ever since King Dunc did die
Things round here have gone awry.
And as if all that was not enough,
The King can't find his friend Macduff.

LORD
Macduff, I hear, is Edward's guest
Down in London getting some rest.
Malcolm, they say, went there on his horse
To try and raise a fighting force.
I hear he's asked for Siward's band,
The fierce man from Northumberland.

Prince Malc would bring the good times back:

A royal feast, not just a snack.

LENNOX

Macbeth has called Macduff back here?

LORD

But he said no . . . for him, I fear!

LENNOX

If you know how to contact him,

You may advise, 'avoid our King,'

And speak to one who's holier

To help save Caledonia!

If anyone asks, we never spoke.

LORD

Don't worry. I'm an honest bloke.

(Exeunt all)

Act IV

SCENE I.

A cavern. In the middle, a boiling cauldron. Thunder.
(Enter the three WITCHES *and* HECATE*)*

FIRST WITCH
Lennox, I think, has started a mission

SECOND WITCH
And we're in this next scene . . .

THIRD WITCH
 . . . So let's get in position.

ALL
Double, double, toil and plight,

HECATE
I hope you don't mess up tonight.

FIRST WITCH
We've put all the ingredients in
From lizard's leg . . .

SECOND WITCH
. . . to owlet's wing.

THIRD WITCH
We'll stir it now and do the dance.

HECATE
And get yourselves into the trance.
And don't you start your own voodoo.
Just stick to what I said to do!

THIRD WITCH
I'm still so cold, can't feel my thumbs.

HECATE
Look out girls, the devil comes . . .

(HECATE *retires*)

(*Enter* MACBETH)

MACBETH
How now, you spirits of the dim!
You see what mess you've got me in?

THIRD WITCH
We didn't say to kill the King.

SECOND WITCH
We didn't say do anything.

MACBETH
Just tell me what will happen next.

FIRST WITCH
We can but try

THIRD WITCH
To do our best.

SECOND WITCH
You want the words from three old witches,
Or prefer to get the news from pictures?

MACBETH
Summon all the spirits here.
But tell me first, who I should fear?

ALL
Come to the land of flu and colds
To show him what the future holds.

(Thunder. First Apparition: a head wearing a helmet.)

FIRST APPARITION
Beware Macduff, the Thane of Fife.

(Descends)

MACBETH
Does he intend to take my life?

FIRST WITCH
Our apparitions[24] come and go.

24—A ghost or vision that tells the future

SECOND WITCH
And that is all you get to know.

(The second apparition: a bloodied child appears)

THIRD WITCH
But have no fear, my little Thane.

FIRST WITCH
The spirits they do come again.

SECOND APPARITION
Laugh you in the face of death.
None born of woman shall harm Macbeth.

(Descends)

MACBETH
None born of woman? No human exists.
But I'll still kill Macduff, cos I just can't resist.

(Thunder. Third Apparition: a Child crowned, with a tree in his hand)

Now what is this strange vision I see?

FIRST WITCH
Behold, our King, it's a kid with a tree!

THIRD APPARITION
Macbeth will live and rule until
Great Birnam moves to Dunsinane Hill.

(Descends)

MACBETH
Go Birnam Wood to Dunsinane?
A forest move? Well that's insane!

(Third Apparition disappears)

I'm liking what I have in store.
Just one last thing . . .

SECOND WITCH
. . . Please ask no more.

THIRD WITCH
'We have to show' is what Hecate said.

FIRST WITCH
Very well, but on your head . . .!

MACBETH
I heard you once but say again . . .
Old Banquo's sons, are they to reign?

(A show of Eight Kings, the last with a mirror in his hand;
GHOST OF BANQUO *following.)*

MACBETH
The ghost of Banquo here does shine,
Followed by a freakish line.
Spirits walking up and down,
Eight of them and all with crown!
All with his resemblance,
I see its ghastly relevance.
Make it stop. Enough I see

Bloody Banquo laughs at me.

SECOND WITCH
He don't look good. Are we in trouble?

THIRD WITCH
Maybe too much hubble-bubble?

FIRST WITCH
We did what Hecate said to do.
The rest, Macbeth, is up to you.

(They make to leave)

MACBETH
You can't leave me with scenes like these.
I'll complain to your authorities.

FIRST WITCH
Feel free, my lord . . .

SECOND WITCH
. . . there's just one hitch.

THIRD WITCH
You just don't know . . .

FIRST WITCH
. . . which witch . . .

SECOND WITCH
. . . is which.

(Music. The witches dance and then vanish, with HECATE*)*

MACBETH
Where have you gone? Come show thy face!
I'm all alone . . .

(Enter LENNOX*)*

LENNOX
. . . Hello, your grace!

MACBETH
Lennox, man, what now? More snags?
Or are you here too to see the hags?

LENNOX
See what hags? I am confused!

MACBETH
So why're you here . . .?

LENNOX
. . . Some men brought news
To England, Lord Macduff did flee.

MACBETH
A stunt like that like I didn't see.
I'll send my finest men to Fife
To kill his kids and kill his wife.

LENNOX
All right, good lord. *(aside)* A bit unkind!

MACBETH
I'm feeling good . . .!

LENNOX
(aside) . . . He's lost his mind.

(Exeunt all)

SCENE II.

Fife. MACDUFF'S *castle.*
(*Enter* WITCHES, LADY MACDUFF, *her* SON, *and* ROSS)

THIRD WITCH
The news from Lennox isn't good.

SECOND WITCH
In Lady Macduff's neighbourhood
It don't look now so tickety-boo

FIRST WITCH
I think we know what Mac will do.

LADY MACDUFF
What had he done, to make him flee?

ROSS
Be patient, ma'am . . .

LADY MACDUFF
 . . . And what about me?

ROSS
Macduff, he left with good intentions.

LADY MACDUFF
Spare your soppy interventions.

He's left us here alone in Fife
To face alone all kinds of strife.
You'll stay with us, my cousin Ross?

ROSS
I can't do that; Macbeth's my boss.

(Exits)

LADY MACDUFF
My son! Your father, is he dead?

SON
He's not! I heard that he's just fled.

LADY MACDUFF
If he has left his family,
Then that man he is dead to me.

(Enter a MESSENGER)

MESSENGER
Excuse me, Lady, barging in.
I saw some men, they're looking grim.
I came to say, if I were you
I'd leave this place . . .

SON
. . . And me?

MESSENGER
. . . You, too!

(Exits)

LADY MACDUFF
But where to go that's any safer?
My life it stands upon a wafer.
Still, we won't now go and cause a fuss.
We'll stay and take what comes to us!

(Enter MURDERERS*)*

FIRST MURDERER
Your husband in . . .?

LADY MACDUFF
 . . . Who wants to know?

SECOND MURDERER
We've come with our respects to show.

SON
You think my dad, Macduff's, a traitor?

LADY MACDUFF
Go to your room, I'll deal with you later!

FIRST MURDERER
Your daddy's gone, my little weed.

SECOND MURDERER
He long ago passed Berwick-'pon-Tweed.

FIRST MURDERER
Now it's just you and your mum.

Get over here and murder 'em.

(Stabbing the SON*)*

SON
Go run away. He's killed me, Mum!

(Dies)

LADY MACDUFF
I'm looking after number one!

(Exit LADY MACDUFF, *crying 'Murder!')*

FIRST MURDERER
You've done it again: one down, one gone.
Macbeth won't like this carrying on.
He was mad enough the first time round.

SECOND MURDERER
Oh shut your hole . . . we'll track her down.

(Exeunt MURDERERS, *following* LADY MACBETH*)*

CENE III.

England. Before the King's palace.

FIRST WITCH
Meanwhile her man's in London town.

SECOND WITCH
And speaks to Malc who just went down.

THIRD WITCH
I think they plan to share their horses
With the imperial English forces.

(Enter MALCOLM *and* MACDUFF*)*

MALCOLM
Well fancy meeting you down here.
I heard you'd run. Are you full of fear?

MACDUFF
If I'd stayed there, then I'd be dead.
I've come to scheme for Macbeth's head.

MALCOLM
Are you sure you're not here to kill me?
You're Macbeth's pal . . . 'tis treachery?

MACDUFF

You think I'd leave my kids and wife
If I wasn't in some kind of strife?
I want him gone, can't say it plainer.
I'll fight with you, it's a no brainer!

MALCOLM

You think I am a worthy heir?

MACDUFF

You've got the wits; you've got the flair.

MALCOLM

Your silver tongue is sweet indeed.
You're now with me. Go get your steed.
Siward's come through with some men.
Together, we'll go north again!

(Enter a DOCTOR*)*

MALCOLM

The English King is on his way?

DOCTOR

He's curing wretched souls today.

MACDUFF

He heals the sick and feeds the poor?

DOCTOR

They're lining up outside his door.
I've got to go . . .

MALCOLM

... You know, Macduff?

When I am king, I'll do that stuff.

(Enter ROSS*)*

MACDUFF

Who now invades our little spot?

MALCOLM

From the way he is dressed, I would say he's a Scot.

MACDUFF

This man, he is no 'dime a dozen'

This is my Ross; a worthy cousin.

(to ROSS*)* I'd thought you'd never come down south!

ROSS

I got some news, from word of mouth:

Scotland goes from bad to worse.

Macbeth is like an evil curse.

The violence that he does awake

Does cause the bravest thane to shake.

The wisest thing is to take flight.

MACDUFF

My wife and kids, are they alright?

ROSS

When I left them, they were fine ... *(hesitantly, looking
down, pulling on his fingers ...)*

MALCOLM

Come on, my lads! It's fighting time!

King Edward's given me his soldiers:

Fierce young men with big, wide shoulders.

ROSS

I'm sorry MacDuff I cannot lie.

She tried to run, but your wife did die.

MACDUFF

I thought you said she's fit and well?

ROSS

She was . . . but then they came from hell.

MacMurderers did take them out.

MALCOLM

This is what I'm talking about!

MACDUFF

My son as well? My little page?[25]

He'll never get to see old age!

MALCOLM

The King is on a killing spree.

But if he can do it, so can we!!

(Exeunt all)

25—(here) a young boy

Act V

SCENE I.

Dunsinane. A small room in MACBETH'S *castle.*

SECOND WITCH
So south of the border, the thanes are talking.

FIRST WITCH
As back at the palace, the Queen's sleepwalking.

(Enter a DOCTOR *and a* MAID)

DOCTOR
You say she walks but is not awake?

MAID
Just take a look, for goodness' sake . . .
She takes a pad and starts to write.

DOCTOR
And all while still asleep . . .?

MAID
. . . That's right!

DOCTOR
Does she speak . . .?

MAID

. . . She does, poor dear.

And here she comes; hide over here!

(Enter LADY MACBETH, *with a candle)*

DOCTOR

From where'd she get that candlelight?

MAID

We have to keep it lit all night

And with it through the night she'll creep.

DOCTOR

Her eyes are awake, her mind asleep!

She rubs her hands with frenzied power.

MAID

For sometimes more than half an hour.

Here she speaks . . .

DOCTOR

. . . We'll see what's what.

I'll write it down . . .

LADY MACBETH

. . . I've missed a spot.

He sure did have a lot of blood.

Too late to nip things in the bud.

The Thane of Fife he had a wife.

Where is she now? She's lost her life . . .

The stench of blood it fills the room.

DOCTOR
That explains the strong perfume!

MAID
Possessed by some almighty beast.

DOCTOR
She don't need me; she needs a priest.

LADY MACBETH
We buried Banquo, don't you fret.
Your crown will last for some time yet.
Another knock! To bed I run.
And dream upon what I've become.

(She exits)

DOCTOR
And now she goes to bed again?

MAID
She does that, sir, and sleeps 'til ten.

DOCTOR
I'll leave, but keep her in your sight.
The visions I did see this night
Do fill my mind with thoughts of dread.
But just for now they'll stay unsaid.

(Exeunt all)

SCENE II.

The country near Dunsinane.

SECOND WITCH
We leave the Queen to what she's contrived.

FIRST WITCH
Cos just near her castle, an army's arrived!

(Sounds of battle drums. Enter MENTEITH, CAITHNESS, ANGUS, LENNOX, *and Soldiers)*

MENTEITH
The English army's close enough
Led by Siward and Macduff.
Siward's fighting son another.

ANGUS
Malcolm too, but not his brother.

LENNOX
This battle will make men of boys.

MENTEITH
You know of Macbeth's fighting ploys?

CAITHNESS
Great Dunsinane he fortifies:

Some say he's mad; some say they're lies.

ANGUS
Well me for one I think he's barmy,[26]
Not sane enough to rule his army!

LENNOX
His prospects now look bleak as hell
I think I'll fight with you as well.

MENTEITH
Me too . . .

CAITHNESS
. . . And me . . .

ANGUS
. . . And I sure will.

LENNOX
Let us now go to Birnam Hill.
We'll march against our former friend
And hope his evil ways to end.

(Exeunt all, marching)

26—Crazy

SCENE III.

Dunsinane. A room in the castle.

THIRD WITCH
The thanes are voting with their feet.

FIRST WITCH
Macbeth's at home, not yet feeling the heat!

(Enter MACBETH, SEYTON *and Attendants)*

MACBETH
It's looking bleak but I don't care.
My predictions mostly set me fair.
Birnam Wood will never move,
And Malc's got a mum; that I can prove.
So all who fear, go, turn, and flee
And leave the loyal folks to me.
Now you can speak and that's an order!

SERVANT
Ten thousand soldiers are on our border . . .

MACBETH
Ten thousand men? I do mishear.
There's not that many men around here.

SERVANT

They've all come up from England, sire.

MACBETH

Get out of here ...!

SERVANT

... It's sounding dire!

(Exit SERVANT*)*

MACBETH

Seyton? Man! For heaven's sake.

This battle will me make or break.

My friends do turn away from me,

But I will fight eternally.

I may not live much more as king,

And maybe that's no bad thing.

SEYTON

It's true, my Lord, what the servants say.

The English are here and your thanes ran away.

I'm sorry my news won't make you feel calmer.

MACBETH

Don't worry 'bout that. Now pass me my armour!

They can fight all they like, but they won't take my life.

(enter DOCTOR*)*

SEYTON

The DOCTOR's here ...

MACBETH

... What news of my wife?

DOCTOR

Her body is fine, but she's looking quite stressed.

And fanciful thoughts do disturb the Queen's rest.

MACBETH

Just give her a drug, something strong off-the-shelf.

DOCTOR

I would do my King, but she must treat herself.

MACBETH

Well if you can't cure 'her indoors',[27]

Cure the English of their wars.

Or give my countrymen some meds

To keep their hearts, not lose their heads.

And death for now I will not fear

Till Birnam comes to Dunsinane near.

DOCTOR

(*aside*) I tell you, if I was free and clear,

Wild horses couldn't drag me here.

(Exeunt all)

27—Slang for wife

SCENE IV.

Country near Birnam Wood.

THIRD WITCH
It's surprising to me that he doesn't feel dread.

SECOND WITCH
That could be to do with the things that we said!

FIRST WITCH
His enemies gathering up near the wood

THIRD WITCH
For Macbeth and his future it doesn't look good!

(*Sound of battle drums. Enter* MALCOLM, SIWARD AND
YOUNG SIWARD, MACDUFF, MENTEITH, CAITHNESS,
ANGUS, LENNOX, ROSS, *and Soldiers, marching*)

MALCOLM
(*to* SIWARD) I'm glad you're here . . .

MENTEITH
. . . You're very good.

MACDUFF
Oh yes you are . . .

SIWARD
. . . Is that a wood?

MENTEITH
That's Birnam Hill.

SIWARD
. . . It's very big.

MALCOLM
Tell every man to grab a twig.
It's camouflage, the latest thing!

MENTEITH
You will make a marvellous king!

SOLDIERS
We did it once and we'll do it again.

SIWARD
Macbeth's alone in Dunsinane?

MALCOLM
He's got some other soldiers there,
But we've got plenty more to spare.

MACDUFF
Let's stop ourselves from counting chickens.
We'll wait to see how this plot thickens.

SIWARD
We'll see what fate has got in store.
Pick up your twigs . . . We go to war!!

(Exeunt, marching)

SCENE V.

Dunsinane. Within the castle.

(Enter MACBETH, SEYTON, and Soldiers, with the sound of battle drums)

THIRD WITCH
The wood looks like it's on the wane.

SECOND WITCH
And back we go to Dunsinane.

MACBETH
Come decorate the castle's wall.
We'll wait right here and kill 'em all.
We'll fight like men, they fight like boys.
Prepare for war . . .

(A cry of women from off stage)

. . . What is that noise?

SEYTON
The cry of women; I'll go and see.

(He exits)

MACBETH
Screams and such do not scare me.

If that's my wife, then let her swoon.
My evil deeds leave me immune.

(Re-enter SEYTON*)*

SEYTON
The Queen, she's dead. She had a fall!

MACBETH
Sooner or later, death takes us all.

SEYTON
It can't just be that black and white!

MACBETH
Life is like a candlelight.
One sec it casts its force about.
The next, a draft will snuff it out.
We are all actors in a play.
We act our life, then pass away.
The lines we spoke and thoughts we had
Are just the musings of the mad.

(Enter a MESSENGER*)*

MESSENGER
Sorry to stop philosophy,
But I just saw a walking tree.

MACBETH
I'll kill you for that crazy talk.

MESSENGER

Birnam Wood has gone for a walk!

I saw on my watch on top of that hill!

But the messenger you shouldn't kill!

MACBETH

This news, it does upset my brain.

The wood it comes to Dunsinane!

If the witches' words were true,

I have nothing left to do.

Come Scottish clouds and block the sun.

At least I'll die with armour on.

SCENE VI.

Dunsinane. Before the castle.

THIRD WITCH
It's hotting up . . .

SECOND WITCH
. . . Which is rare up here.

THIRD WITCH
In front of the castle, will a hero appear?

(Sound of battle drums. Enter MALCOLM, SIWARD, YOUNG
SIWARD, MACDUFF, *and their Army, with boughs)*

MALCOLM
There's his castle, Dunsinane.
Now drop the twigs and show him plain
His enemy is very large.
Siward and son, you lead the charge.
Macduff and I will follow you.

SIWARD
I hope you will . . .

YOUNG SIWARD
. . . You'd better do!

MACDUFF

Let trumpets call and grab your arms
Let's go and get the Thane of Glamis.

(Exeunt all)

 SCENE VII.

Another part of the field.

THIRD WITCH
The Thane of Glamis has left his fort.

SECOND WITCH
But he needs to look out or he may be caught!

(Fighting noises. Enter MACBETH*)*

MACBETH
They're on the move and nearly here.
Those not born to woman are all that I fear.

(Enter YOUNG SIWARD*)*

YOUNG SIWARD
What is your name?

MACBETH
. . . You know not my face?
This is my country, my home, and my place!

YOUNG SIWARD
Macbeth? The King! . . . Come draw your sword.

MACBETH
I'll kill you here, you have my word.

YOUNG SIWARD
The devil will not take this lad . . .

(They fight, SIWARD is injured)

MACBETH
That's got to hurt . . .

YOUNG SIWARD
 . . . It's pretty bad!

(YOUNG SIWARD is slain)

MACBETH
You were born of a woman, now that is clear.
The witches were right, I've nothing to fear!

(He exits. Sounds of fighting. Enter MACDUFF)

MACDUFF
I hope Macbeth lives long enough
For him to be killed by me, Macduff.

(Enter MALCOLM and SIWARD)

SIWARD
My lord, the battle's almost won.
Our men do fight . . .

MALCOLM

... His men do run.

He doesn't pay them enough per hour

To overcome our firepower!

SIWARD

I just got word the castle's breached.

MALCOLM

I think the final scene we've reached!

(Exeunt. Sounds of fighting)

SCENE VIII.

Another part of the field.

THIRD WITCH
Malcolm is right, just one more to go . . .

SECOND WITCH
We'll soon see what gives at the end of the show.

FIRST WITCH
Will our predictions hold their own?

SECOND WITCH
Just two more minutes and all will be known!

(Enter MACBETH*)*

MACBETH
My chance to win looks less than zero.
But I'll fight to the end, not like that Nero.

(Enter MACDUFF*)*

MACDUFF
Turn around, you hound from hell!

MACBETH
That voice: Macduff, I know it well.

I have till now avoided you,
But now you're here I'll run you through.

MACDUFF
Bring it on, you evil villain.
I still have appetite for killin'.

(They fight)

MACBETH
You cannot win, your hopes are forlorn.
You are from a woman born.

MACDUFF
You are wrong, barbarian!
I was born Caesarean![28]

MACBETH
You tell me this, I lose my edge.

MACDUFF
Come back here. I give this pledge
Your soul in hell it may be cursed
But to stay alive will be much worse!

MACBETH
The wood it moved, you're not from birth,
My time is short upon this earth.
The hags I blame for what I've become,
But it's too late now, let's get this done!

28—A Caesarean birth is a surgery where the baby is removed by cutting the mother's body.

(Both exit, fighting. Sounds of fighting. A retreat. Then a trumpet flourish. Enter, with drums, MALCOLM, SIWARD, ROSS, *the other Thanes, and Soldiers)*

MALCOLM
We've won, but many friends we've lost.

SIWARD
It's not that bad; we'll count the cost.
The major thing is we've had fun.

MALCOLM
Macduff is missing, and your son.

ROSS
Your son is dead . . .!

SIWARD
. . . Oh please don't say
Do we know how . . .?

ROSS
. . . The hero's way.

SIWARD
Then I am proud he was my son,
Stiff upper lip; my mourning's done!

(Re-enter MACDUFF, *with* MACBETH'S *head)*

MACDUFF
Revenging Banquo and Fleance

And all the rest . . . I bring his bonce![29]
He'll reign no more as Scottish king.

ROSS
Looks like he won't do anything.

MACDUFF
The King is dead, the new one's here.

SIWARD
Let's all go and grab a beer.

MALCOLM
Will you take us to some drinking spots?

MACDUFF
Anything for the King of the Scots!

(Trumpet fanfare. They exeunt)

WITCHES
Hubble, bubble, toil and plot.

FIRST WITCH
He had it all and lost the lot.

THIRD WITCH
Macbeth has gone, his Queen she died.
I'm told that it was suicide.

SECOND WITCH
Don't hate us now we're not to blame.

29—Head

THIRD WITCH

I think there's something 'bout his name

WITCHES

And so it ends our play, *Macbeth,*

A name that always rhymes with DEATH!

More Drama Resources from Alphabet Publishing

Silly Shakespeare for Students by Paul Leonard Murray

A Midsummer Night's Dream

Pericles

Short Original Plays by Alice Savage

Just Desserts: A foodie drama about a chef gone bad

Introducing Rob: Lola's family loves her new boyfriend. Until they actually meet him

Colorado Ghost Story: Two exchange students get into trouble in the old West

Strange Medicine: Who decides what the truth is?

The Drama Book: Lesson Plans, Activities, and Scripts for the English Language Classroom by Alice Savage

ISTD Coursebooks by Alice Savage

The Integrated Skills Through Drama coursebooks contain a complete curriculum built around an original one-act play. Aimed at intermediate learners, teenagers and older.

Her Own Worst Enemy: A serious comedy about choosing a major

Only the Best Intentions: A love triangle between a guy, a girl and a game

Rising Water: A stormy drama about what happens to people in a crisis

Alphabet Publishing is an independent publisher of creative and innovative educational material. All of our resources were conceived and created by teachers working in the classroom. We support our creators by giving them creative control and by sharing profits. Learn more about us and our resources at www.alphabetpublish.com

Printed in Great Britain
by Amazon